The Importance of Spiritual Understanding
Bisi Oladipupo

Springs of life publishing

Copyright © 2024 by Bisi Oladipupo

Springs of life publishing

ISBN: 978-1-915269-42-3 (ePub e-book)

ISBN: 978-1-915269-43-0 (paperback)

All Rights Reserved.

No part of this book may be used or reproduced by any means, graphic, electronic, or mechanical, including photocopying, recording, taping, or by any information storage retrieval system without the written permission of the publisher except in the case of brief quotations embodied in critical articles and reviews.

Printed in the United Kingdom

Unless otherwise indicated, scripture quotations are taken from the New King James Version.

Scripture taken from the New King James Version®. Copyright © 1982 by Thomas Nelson. Used by permission. All rights reserved.

Scripture quotations from The Authorized (King James) Version. Rights in the Authorized Version in the United Kingdom are vested in the Crown. Reproduced by permission of the Crown's patentee, Cambridge University Press.

Scripture quotations marked (AMP) are taken from the Amplified Bible, Copyright © 2015 by The Lockman Foundation. Used by permission.

Contents

Dedication	IV
Introduction	V
1. What is Spiritual Understanding	1
2. How Do We Get Spiritual Understanding?	6
3. Examples of Areas Where We Need Spiritual Understanding	10
4. Application of Spiritual Understanding	32
5. Conclusion	36
Salvation Prayer	39
About the author	40
Also by Bisi	41

To Jesus Christ my Lord and Saviour; to Him alone that laid down His life that I might have life eternal. To Him that led captivity captive and gave gifts unto men (Ephesians 4; 8). One of those gifts is writing!

Bisi Oladipupo

Introduction

In the natural, a person is likely not to maximise the opportunity, circumstance, or thing without understanding.

Have you ever seen a parent try to insist their child goes to school? If possible, the child just wants to play games and doesn't want to do homework or go to school.

This is why some countries legally require children up to a certain age to attend school. This is because these countries know the impact of raising children who will not be able to read or write in the future.

The same applies to our Christian walk.

Without spiritual understanding, we will live our Christian walk with severe limitations. This is one reason why our prayer meetings are the least attended. A lack of spiritual understanding affects believers in a wide variety of ways.

Spiritual understanding is so important that Paul prayed for it in one of his prayers:

*"For this reason we also, since the day we heard it, do not cease to pray for you, and to ask that you may be filled **with the knowledge of His will in all wisdom and spiritual understanding;** ^{10} that you may walk worthy of the Lord, fully pleasing Him, being fruitful in every good work and increasing in the knowledge of God"* (Colossians 1:9-10).

According to the above scripture, it takes "wisdom and spiritual understanding" to walk worthy of the Lord, fully pleasing Him.

This book will examine "spiritual understanding", why we need it, and how it will enhance our walk in Christ.

Be blessed!

Chapter 1
What is Spiritual Understanding

The spirit realm is real.

God's kingdom is a real kingdom, but we don't see it in the natural. It is spiritual and can manifest in our natural world in a variety of ways.

Jesus told His disciples to tell the people when they heal the sick: *"The kingdom of God is come nigh unto you"* (Luke 10:9). This is simply a manifestation of the kingdom of God, which we cannot see with our natural eyes.

So, what is spiritual understanding? To put it in simple terms, it simply means spiritual reasoning, implications, and full appreciation of the spiritual reason and weight of a matter.

Why do some people not gladly embrace the good news of the gospel and receive Jesus Christ as their Lord and Saviour?

The main reason is a lack of spiritual understanding. If people really knew how desperate they need the Lord, the love and great plans He has for them, what living in God's kingdom is all about, and the unspeakable eternal rewards that await those who serve the Lord, everyone would run to Him.

It is God's goodness that leads a man to repentance. Yes, hell is a real place, but nobody needs to go there. Unfortunately, people do, but there is no need for it; so far as a person receives Jesus Christ, the lover of their souls, as Lord and Saviour.

Can we see why spiritual understanding is so important?

It takes understanding to be converted.

"*For this people's heart is waxed gross, and their ears are dull of hearing, and their eyes they have closed; lest at any time they should see with their eyes and hear with their ears, and **should understand with their heart**, and should be converted, and I should heal them* (Matthew 13:15).

This principle of understanding applies in all areas of our walk with Christ.

Why do we have to plead with some Christians to read their Bibles? Why are so many prayer meetings the least attended? Why do Christians think they can have one foot in the world

THE IMPORTANCE OF SPIRITUAL UNDERSTANDING

and another in the kingdom? The root problem with many of these characteristics is a lack of spiritual understanding.

It is best to simply know that God loves us and whatever He instructs us to do is for our own good. It is a good foundational truth and understanding that will propel us in our walk with the Lord.

Poor decisions are made when a person lacks spiritual understanding.

As mentioned before, it is so important that it is a requirement to walk worthy of the Lord unto all pleasing (Colossians 1:9-10).

We can see a classic example of a person who made a poor decision in the gospels—the rich young man. The Lord asked this man to sell all he had and follow Him, but the rich man turned down the offer.

*"Jesus said to him, "If you want to be perfect, go, sell what you have and give to the poor, and **you will have treasure in heaven; and come, follow Me."***

²² But when the young man heard that saying, he went away sorrowful, for he had great possessions" (Matthew 19:21-22).

What a great opportunity this young man missed!

If he had spiritual understanding, he would not have turned down such a great offer. After all, where would be the best place to invest? On earth that is temporal, or in heaven that is eternal? He also missed being mentored by Jesus Christ. Jesus said, *"Come, follow me"*, and he turned it down.

That is just one example of the gross consequence of lacking spiritual understanding. Only heaven knows what this young, rich man missed. Before throwing stones at this young man, we must be careful not to trade temporal things for eternal rewards.

On the other hand, we have many examples of those who made good decisions. The Lord equally told many of His disciples, *"Follow me"*, and they left everything and followed Him.

"And Jesus, walking by the sea of Galilee, saw two brethren, Simon called Peter, and Andrew his brother, casting a net into the sea: for they were fishers.

*[19] And he saith unto them, **Follow me, and I will make you fishers of men**.*

*[20] And they **straightway left their nets, and followed him*** (Matthew 4:18-20; KJV).

*After these things He went out and saw a tax collector named Levi, sitting at the tax office. And He said to him, **"Follow Me."** [28] **So he left all, rose up, and followed Him*** (Luke 5:27-28).

THE IMPORTANCE OF SPIRITUAL UNDERSTANDING

Isn't this beautiful? Just look at the responses of Peter, Simon, and Levi. Levi is also known as Matthew (Matthew 9:9), one of the twelve disciples (Matthew 10:2-4). Did you realise that any of them could have said no? Now, let us take a peek at one of their eternal rewards:

The foundation of the walls of the new Jerusalem has the names of the twelve apostles of the Lamb.

"Now the wall of the city had twelve foundations, and on them were the [j]names of the twelve apostles of the Lamb" (Revelation 21:14).

What an amazing eternal reward!

Chapter 2

How Do We Get Spiritual Understanding?

So, how do we get spiritual understanding?

Scripture tells us to apply our hearts to understanding (Proverbs 2:2). In other words, spiritual understanding will not just drop on us.

Firstly, we must know that God's word is the truth, and we must apply our hearts to the Word of God. This is done by reading, studying, and meditating on the word of God. Before we open our Bibles, we should pray and ask the Holy Spirit to give us revelation. God's word is spirit and life (John 6:63).

By applying our hearts to the Word of God, we apply our hearts to spiritual understanding. True understanding is of the heart (Matthew 13:15). If we spend our time playing computer games and social media and do not invest enough time in God's Word, it will impact the level of our spiritual understanding. This is one reason the scriptures tell us to *"guard our hearts with all diligence"* (Proverbs 4:23).

Another way to get spiritual understanding is to ask for it. We can find a prayer for spiritual understanding in the Book of Colossians:

"*For this reason we also, since the day we heard it, do not cease to pray for you, and to ask that you may be filled with the knowledge of His will in all wisdom and spiritual understanding;* **10** *that you may walk worthy of the Lord, fully pleasing Him, being fruitful in every good work and increasing in the knowledge of God*" (Colossians 1:9-10).

Just observing life in light of Scripture can also bring us spiritual understanding:

"If I had said, "I will speak thus,"Behold, I would have been untrue to the generation of Your children.**16** When I thought *how* to understand this,It *was* [e]too painful for me—**17** Until I went into the sanctuary of God;*Then* I understood their end" (Psalm 73:15-17).

"I went by the field of the lazy *man*,And by the vineyard of the man devoid of understanding;**31** And there it was, all overgrown with thorns;Its surface was covered with nettles;Its stone wall was broken down.**³²** When I saw *it,* I considered *it* well;**I looked on *it and* received instruction:³³** A little sleep, a little slumber,A little folding of the hands to rest;**³⁴** So shall your poverty come *like* [f]a prowler,And your need like [g]an armed man" (Proverbs 24:30-34).

Meditating on God's Word also brings spiritual understanding.

"I have more understanding than all my teachers,For Your testimonies are my meditation" (Psalm 119:99).

What understanding is David speaking about here? It is safe to say that David is referring to spiritual understanding. If David's teachers are only providing him natural information, as is typical in public schools today, then meditating on God's word will give us greater understanding, including spiritual understanding.

The Holy Spirit is the Spirit of truth, and He is ever ready to give us understanding. Sometimes, we can deal with a spiritual matter from a natural point of view if we do not rely on the Holy Spirit to make us understand what is really happening. A good example would be dealing with a difficult person. In the natural, we might see a complicated person; however, spiritual understanding might reveal the root of rejection. It could be that the person has gone through difficult times in life, and these

THE IMPORTANCE OF SPIRITUAL UNDERSTANDING

have affected the person, which is now manifesting in other relationships.

Spiritual understanding will help you not to take it personally but rather pray for the person. You might be able to help the person if you have access to them and are given authority and permission to speak into their lives. Can we see how spiritual understanding makes a difference?

Listening to the inner witness is also part of our access to spiritual understanding. The Holy Spirit bears witness with our spirits that we are children of God (Romans 8:16). He also bears witness to other things in our daily walk. The scriptures tell us to walk in the Spirit (Galatians 5:16). Therefore, we must walk with a spiritual understanding of what we receive about a matter because that is the real truth of the situation.

Spiritual understanding is accessed by faith. We must apply our hearts to the reality of God's truth.

Chapter 3
Examples of Areas Where We Need Spiritual Understanding

Our Salvation

Having a spiritual understanding of what took place at the new birth, when we received Jesus Christ as our Lord and Saviour, is a lifetime journey. However, it is essential to understand spiritually what took place.

This is why the discipleship and mentoring of new believers in Christ are vital. This book will not fully explore what takes place at the new birth. However, it is one of the most important decisions anyone will make because it affects both this life and the life to come.

THE IMPORTANCE OF SPIRITUAL UNDERSTANDING

Here are a few things that took place at the new birth:

A person becomes a new creation in Christ Jesus (2 Corinthians 5:17).

A person's spirit becomes new in Christ Jesus. Our salvation only affects our spirits. Hence, we have to renew our minds, allow God's word to save our souls, and discipline our bodies. Some people have glorious encounters at salvation, and habits supernaturally break off. In fact, deliverances take place; however, this is not necessarily every other person's experience.

The believer will have to renew their minds and work out their salvation with fear and trembling. What does that mean? It simply means we need to cooperate with the person of the Holy Spirit to allow what has happened on the inside to manifest in the physical realm.

*"Wherefore lay apart all filthiness and superfluity of naughtiness, **and receive with meekness the engrafted word, which is able to save your souls**"* (James 1:21).

We can see from this passage of Scripture that the Word of God is able to save our souls.

Who hath delivered us from the power of darkness, and translated us into the kingdom of his dear Son (Colossians 1:13).

What a great privilege at the new birth! At the point of receiving Jesus Christ as Lord and Saviour, *a person is moved into another kingdom*. This kingdom is a spiritual kingdom, and it is important that we become aware of what belongs to us in this new kingdom and how it works.

But as many as received him, to them gave he power to become the sons of God, even to them that believe on his name: (John 1:12).

What another wonderful privilege! *A person becomes a child of God* after receiving Him as Lord and Saviour. Could this be one reason the angels of heaven rejoice over the conversation of one sinner (Luke 15:7)? In the natural, there is rejoicing when a child is born, which applies spiritually, too.

As believers in Christ, we need to understand that we are now children of God.

We are one spirit with Christ

As believers in Christ, we are one spirit with the Lord. This is why we need to walk worthy of the Lord.

*Or do you not know that he who is joined to a harlot is one body **with her**? For "the two," He says, "shall become one flesh." ^{17} But he who is joined to the Lord is one spirit **with Him*** (1 Corinthians 6:16-17).

THE IMPORTANCE OF SPIRITUAL UNDERSTANDING

The scriptures tell us to walk worthy of the Lord (Colossians 1:10).

Translated into the Kingdom of His dear Son

When we give our lives to the Lord, we are actually delivered from the power of darkness and translated into another kingdom.

"Giving thanks unto the Father, which hath made us meet to be partakers of the inheritance of the saints in light: Who hath delivered us from the power of darkness, and hath translated us into the kingdom of his dear Son:" (Colossians 1:12-13).

There are so many spiritual realities that take place at new birth. It is a good idea to explore these from the scriptures so that we are aware of what now belongs to us in Christ. This will be an anchor for us in our Christian walk.

Our Words

Our words are crucial, and being ignorant of them can be very costly. The scriptures tell us that death and life are in the power of the tongue (Proverbs 18:21).

We must be careful with our words. We must not allow the enemy to use our words against us. When we speak contrary to what is truth in God's Word, or even when we speak about others not around us, which is not in line with God's truth, we need to repent and nullify those words in Jesus' Name.

The Nature of God

Have you ever heard someone say something that does not represent God's nature?

It is important to know the nature of God. Unfortunately, there are times when people misrepresent Him.

"The thief cometh not, but for to steal, and to kill, and to destroy: I am come that they might have life, and that they might have it more abundantly" (John 10:10).

Anything that steals, kills, or destroys is not God. Jesus is the express image of the Father (Hebrews 1:3), and He came to give life more abundantly.

This understanding will help us stand against what needs to be stood against and refused.

We will mention a few other attributes of the Lord.

God is love (1 John 4:16).

God is faithful (1 Corinthians 1:10).

God is patient (Romans 15:5).

THE IMPORTANCE OF SPIRITUAL UNDERSTANDING

The Lord is righteous (1 John 2:29).

These are just a few of the attributes of God's nature.

We need a good understanding of His nature in our Christian walk. That way, we will rest in the character of God and interpret anything that happens through who the Lord is, not lies.

Eternal Rewards

If believers knew the rewards of following the will of God for their lives, many would not have a complacent attitude.

Begging people to seek the Lord, obey Him, and submit to what He wants is just a symptom of a lack of spiritual understanding.

Paul said it this way, *"I have fought a good fight, I have finished my course, I have kept the faith:* ***⁸ Henceforth there is laid up for me a crown of righteousness****, which the Lord, the righteous judge, shall give me at that day: and not to me only, but unto all them also that love his appearing"* (2 Timothy 4:7-8; KJV).

From this scripture, we can tell that Paul knew that "a crown of righteousness" was waiting for him. How many times do we hear this preached?

The Book of James speaks about a crown of life for those who endure temptation (James 1:12). The Lord told the disciples of their rewards during His earthly ministry (Matthew 19:28). In the Book of Revelation, we can also see many rewards for those who serve the Lord.

He who overcomes will have access to the tree of life (Revelation 2:7).

He who overcomes will be a pillar in the temple of God, and Jesus Himself will write upon the person the Lord's new name and other rewards (Revelation 3:12).

He who overcomes will be seated with Jesus on His throne (Revelation 3:21).

Here are just a few rewards.

There are things to overcome in this world if we follow the Lord fully. We can be assured that nothing compares to the rewards for those who fully follow the Lord.

Salvation is free, but rewards are earned.

Loving the Lord with all our hearts and having spiritual understanding can help us make better choices and decisions in this present world.

Eternal Consequences

The word "Hell" is not mentioned today in many sermons. However, the truth remains that hell is a real place for those who

THE IMPORTANCE OF SPIRITUAL UNDERSTANDING

do receive the sacrifice of Jesus Christ by accepting and making Him Lord of their lives.

The word "hell" is mentioned twenty-three times in the New Testament. During the earthly ministry of Jesus, the Lord mentioned the word "hell".

"But I will show you whom you should fear: Fear Him who, after He has killed, has power to cast into hell; yes, I say to you, fear Him!" (Luke 12:5).

And the sea gave up the dead which were in it; and death and hell delivered up the dead which were in them: and they were judged every man according to their works. ^{14} And death and hell were cast into the lake of fire. This is the second death. **And whosoever was not found written in the book of life** *was cast into the lake of fire* (Revelation 20:13-15; KJV).

Someone once said, "everyone is eternal". It does not matter how people look on the outside, whether they are well-dressed, have fancy cars, or live in large and great houses. Everyone is everlasting and will depart this earth one day, except the Lord returns.

This understanding will ensure that we share the gospel with others. Whenever we have a prompting, we must respond, because we don't know if it is the last chance to speak to the person.

Once, I listened to an account by a certain man of God. In summary, he said that he had an urge to minister and share Christ with a particular person, but he did not.

Later that evening, he was about to minister and decided to pray before the meeting. As he knelt to pray, he had a vision and saw the person he was supposed to share Christ with in hell.

The Lord told him, *"I will hold you accountable on that day for this man because you did not obey me"*.

He was unable to preach that evening, so he had to delegate it to someone else to speak in his place.

This is the seriousness of not sharing the gospel, especially if it is a person's last chance, and only the Lord will know that.

Heaven is a real place. While many have referred to the Book of Revelation as an end-time affair book, the reality is that we can see so much of what heaven looks like.

The foundations of the heavenly Jerusalem are garnished with all manner of precious stones (Revelation 21:18–20). There is a pure river of water proceeding from the throne of God (Revelation 22:1). The city is pure gold (Revelation 21:18). No more pain, death, or crying (Revelation 21:4). This is just a little description of the heavenly Jerusalem. What a place to spend eternity!

THE IMPORTANCE OF SPIRITUAL UNDERSTANDING

The role of the Holy Spirit in the believer's life

As believers in Christ, we must understand the role of the person of the Holy Spirit in our lives. He is the one who has come to help us and be with us forever (John 14:16). We have to acknowledge His role in our lives.

How often do we do things our way and even go through unnecessary challenges because we have not asked for help or learnt how to engage the Holy Spirit in our day-to-day activities?

I would encourage you to get the book by Bisi Oladipupo, *The Person of the Holy Spirit*, as we cannot deal with all the roles He plays in this book.

We must get to the place in our walk with the Lord where we are confident that the Holy Spirit speaks to us or guides us in a certain direction.

I watched a Christian TV interview recently, and you could tell that the person interviewed was so confident in his walk with the Holy Spirit.

This should be the experience of every believer.

He is already with us, and we just have to learn to engage Him.

We walk by faith; therefore, it will take steps of faith to walk and experience the great role the Holy Spirit plays in our lives.

I challenge you to study more about who the Holy Spirit is and how He has been sent to help us.

Why we need to pray

Have you ever asked yourself why we need to pray? Does the Lord need me to ask?

Well, there are many reasons why we need to pray, and it is important that we understand our need for prayer.

Firstly, God has given us free will. Therefore, we must invite the Lord into our lives, which is why we need to pray.

Whosoever calls upon the name of the Lord shall be saved (Romans 10:13). According to this scripture, a person has to call before they can be saved. This is a form of prayer. The Lord is ready to save (Isaiah 38:20) and wants all men to be saved (1 Timothy 2:4), but it is up to man to call upon the Lord. This simply shows how important prayer is. We initiated the receiving of our salvation by praying and asking for it.

Most other things in the kingdom of God work like that. We have to pray.

One part of the full armour of God stated in the Book of Ephesians is prayer.

THE IMPORTANCE OF SPIRITUAL UNDERSTANDING

"Praying always with all prayer and supplication in the Spirit, being watchful to this end with all perseverance and supplication for all the saints" (Ephesians 6:18).

We have an enemy, and prayer is part of the full armour of God that has been given to us. We do have to pray.

Saul, known as Paul, had a greater encounter when he met the Lord on the road to Damascus (Act 9:1-8). Despite receiving a great ministry, Paul still asked for prayers:

"*And for me, that utterance may be given to me, that I may open my mouth boldly to make known the mystery of the gospel, **20** for which I am an ambassador in chains; that in it I may speak boldly, as I ought to speak* (Ephesians 6:19-20).

Have you been given a prophetic word? You might need to wage good warfare for it to come to pass. Paul here is speaking to Timothy:

"This [f]charge I commit to you, son Timothy, according to the prophecies previously made concerning you, that by them you may wage the good warfare" (1 Timothy 1:18).

Why "good warfare"? Because God is on our side, and He just needs us to engage Him as we live in a fallen world.

Prayer is crucial because we have an enemy and must establish the victory we have in Christ Jesus.

Jesus, during His earthly ministry, prayed all night to the Father (Luke 6:12).

If Jesus prayed, then we also need to pray.

There are different types of prayer, but this book will not address that. However, we must emphasise the importance of prayer. When we have a spiritual understanding of why we need to pray, we will take our prayer lives very seriously.

The Scripture tells us to pray and not faint (Luke 18:1).

We are now the Body of Christ (1 Corinthians 12:27), and Jesus is the head of the body (Colossians 1:18). We are the ones on earth who need to take the authority Jesus has given us to establish God's kingdom here. Part of this involves prayer, as we see when Jesus taught His disciples how to pray.

Thy kingdom come, thy will be done on the earth, as it is in heaven (Matthew 6:10). We can also see that it takes prayer to establish the will of God on earth. Jesus gave us a hint when He included it in what we call "The Lord's prayer".

I remember an encounter that a man of God had many years ago. He had a vision of the Lord, and Jesus spoke to him about some things. During the conversation, a demon got between him and Jesus, and he could no longer hear what Jesus was saying.

THE IMPORTANCE OF SPIRITUAL UNDERSTANDING

In his mind, he was thinking, *"Doesn't Jesus know that l can no longer hear what He is saying? When is the Lord going to do something about it?"* After a while, this man of God commanded the demon to leave in Jesus' name, and it left. This man then asked Jesus, *"Why did you do anything about it?"*

Jesus responded that He had already done everything that needed to be done about our enemy, and we are the ones who have to take our authority.

This simply explains the importance of prayer. We do have to pray.

All we need to do is go through Scripture and see the amazing responses to prayer. We can also see where man did not involve God and the consequences.

Joshua is a good example. Their neighbours acted like strangers because they did not want Israel to fight with them.

They fooled Joshua simply because he and the leaders did not seek counsel from the Lord.

"*14 Then the men of Israel took some of their provisions; but they [e]did not ask counsel of the Lord. 15 So Joshua made peace with them, and made a covenant with them to let them live; and the rulers of the congregation swore to them.*

¹⁶ And it happened at the end of three days, after they had made a covenant with them, that they heard that they were their neighbors who dwelt near them. ¹⁷ Then the children of Israel journeyed and came to their cities on the third day. Now their cities were Gibeon, Chephirah, Beeroth, and Kirjath Jearim. ¹⁸ But the children of Israel did not [f] attack them, because the rulers of the congregation had sworn to them by the Lord God of Israel. And all the congregation complained against the rulers" (Joshua 9:14-18).

Could some things have been avoided if we prayed?

Praying in the Spirit

Praying in the Spirit is a great privilege that believers in Christ have today. The Scripture tells us: *But you, beloved, building yourselves up on your most holy faith, praying in the Holy Spirit* (Jude 1:20).

When we pray in the Spirit, we are building up and edifying ourselves (1 Corinthians 14:4). This is one advantage of praying in the Spirit. As believers in Christ, we cannot afford our minds to talk us out of this great privilege because our minds are unfruitful. In other words, our minds do not know what is going on; however, our spirits are praying (1 Corinthians 14:14). The scriptures also tell us that we are speaking unto God and speaking mysteries (1 Corinthians 14:2). Can you imagine speaking to God only about what He understands? This is what praying in the Spirit is about.

Why would any believer in Christ not want to take advantage of a direct line to God? In the natural, our minds and understanding are limited. We may have our prayer lists, prayer points, and what we know in the natural, but only the Lord knows what we really need to pray about. Things unknown to us. This is the advantage we have when we pray in the Spirit.

The Book of Romans puts it this way:

"Likewise the Spirit also helps in our weaknesses. For we do not know what we should pray for as we ought, but the Spirit Himself makes intercession [g] for us with groanings which cannot be uttered. 27 Now He who searches the hearts knows what the mind of the Spirit is, because He makes intercession for the saints according to the will of God" (Romans 8:26-27).

We can see from this scripture that the Holy Spirit is helping us pray for God's will. So, why do some believers not apply this great privilege we have in Christ? One reason is simply a lack of spiritual understanding. The mind might be saying, *"What is going on?"* However, a person who has spiritual understanding and knows what praying in the Spirit is all about will persevere and reap great rewards.

Our position in Christ

Once we get saved, it is so important to understand our position in Christ. We have already explained what happens to us when we get saved. But did you know there is much more to know after our salvation?

The Scripture reads, *"Who will have all men to be saved, and to come unto the knowledge of the truth"* (1 Timothy 2:4).

Notice that after being saved, we need to come to the knowledge of the truth. It is not an overnight journey, but we must start somewhere.

Once we are saved, we are in Christ (2 Corinthians 5:17). Therefore, we have to know what belongs to us in Christ. This is what will cause us to walk in great spiritual authority, because it is all about Him.

I recommend you go through the epistles and discover who we are in Christ.

Here are a few scriptures you can meditate on:

"And raised us up together, and made us sit together in the heavenly places in Christ Jesus" (Ephesians 2:6).

When God raised Jesus from the dead, we were raised with Him. We can now pray from that place of authority.

THE IMPORTANCE OF SPIRITUAL UNDERSTANDING

"In Him we have redemption through His blood, the forgiveness of sins, according to the riches of His grace" (Ephesians 1:7).

We have redemption through the blood of Christ Jesus. We have been redeemed from the curse of the law (Galatians 3:13). We have been redeemed unto God and now made priests and kings (Revelation 5:10). Here are just a few things we have been redeemed from.

"But to us there is but one God, the Father, of whom are all things, and we in him; and one Lord Jesus Christ, by whom are all things, and we by him" (1 Corinthians 8:6; KJV).

The scriptures tell us that we are in Him. Whatever we do, we need to see ourselves in Him. Wrapped up in Him. We are not walking this race in our own strength. Christ lives in us (Colossians 1:27).

The Word of God

It is quite important that we have a spiritual understanding of the Word of God. This is vital for a vibrant walk in Christ.

Did you know that Jesus Christ is the Word of God (Revelation 19:13)?

When we meditate on the Word of God, we are meditating on Jesus Christ. The Word of God is living and powerful (Hebrews 4:12; AMP).

God's Word is a tangible substance. This is the reality of God's Word. The scriptures tell us that God's Word is the sword of the Spirit (Ephesians 6:17). In the natural, is a sword real? Yes, a sword is real and tangible. Therefore, God's Word is real, tangible, and a fighting tool in the spirit realm.

Could this be one of the reasons people are fighting spiritual wars with carnal weapons? It won't work. God's Word is the sword of the Spirit, and every battle needs appropriate and applicable weapons to deal with it. The Bible tells us that the weapons of our warfare are not carnal (2 Corinthians 10:4).

The Scripture also tells us to allow the word of Christ to dwell in us richly (Colossians 3:16). If someone approached you and asked to come and stay with you, what would come to mind? A physical person staying with you—that is, dwelling with you. Letting the Word of Christ dwell in you richly tells us that "the word of Christ" is an actual substance. A spiritual substance that is real.

The Word of God is quick and powerful (Hebrews 4:12). Another version of the Bible says this:

*"For the word of God is **living and active** and full of power [making it operative, energizing, and effective]. It is sharper than any two-edged [b]sword, penetrating as far as the division of the [c]soul and spirit [the completeness of a person], and of both joints*

THE IMPORTANCE OF SPIRITUAL UNDERSTANDING

and marrow [the deepest parts of our nature], exposing and judging the very thoughts and intentions of the heart" (Hebrews 4:12).

Natural electricity is alive and powerful, and it is a substance. God's Word is powerful, and it is a spiritual substance. When we know the Word of God for what it really is, there will be no more pleas to read our Bibles, meditate on God's word, and lay it in our hearts, as we already have a spiritual understanding of what God's Word is.

In the Book of Matthew, we are told that man shall not live by bread alone.

"But He answered and said, "It is written, 'Man shall not live by bread alone, but by every word that proceeds from the mouth of God' (Matthew 4:4).

To live by bread, we need to eat it physically, pursue it, and buy it. The same actually applies to God's Word. It is spiritual food, and meditating on God's Word is one way of eating and digesting it as a person would eat natural food. We buy God's Word with our time—time that we invest it in.

Buy the truth and sell it not (Proverbs 23:23).

I counsel thee to buy of me gold tried in the fire, that thou mayest be rich (Revelation 3:18).

Jesus said He is the bread of life (John 6:35).

Jesus told Peter "come", and he walked on water (Matthew 14:29). Peter walked on "come" from the mouth of Jesus.

We have just looked at a few examples from Scripture that show that God's Word is an actual tangible spiritual substance that can never fail (Isaiah 55:11).

Our enemy

We do have an enemy called the devil. It is important that we are aware of his devices. The Scripture tells us that we are not ignorant of his devices (2 Corinthians 2:11). The Scripture also tells us to give him no place (Ephesians 4:27). He is called the "wicked one" (1 John 5:18), a liar (John 8:44), and the one who deceives the whole world (Revelation 12:9).

We are to be sober-minded and give the enemy no place. Thieves normally take advantage of people when they are not vigilant. The Bible tells us to be sober and vigilant (1 Peter 5:8). We cannot afford to live careless lives, as we have an enemy seeking any opportunity he can find. This is why we must abide in the vine, keep ourselves in the love of God, be fortified in God's Word, live holy lives, and walk as close to the Lord as we know how.

We must learn to bring every thought captive to the obedience of Christ (2 Corinthians 10:5), resist lies, and know the truth. God's word is truth and part of the armour the Lord has given us to stand against the enemy (Ephesians 6:14). We must know the weapons that the Lord has given us and who we are in Christ.

The good news is that our fight of faith is called "the good fight of faith" (1 Timothy 6:12), while warfare is "wage a good warfare" (1 Timothy 1:18). Why do we have the word "good" attached to both words? Because we are just enforcing the victory that we already have in Christ. We are more than conquerors through Him who loved us (Romans 8:37).

Chapter 4
Application of Spiritual Understanding

Spiritual understanding will help us make informed decisions in this life. In some cases, it will also help us refuse to yield to the flesh or take the carnal path. It is pertinent to know that walking in carnality is very costly.

We have looked at the importance of spiritual understanding in a few examples of our Christian walk, which also highlights the importance of discipleship. Young believers in Christ need to be taught and discipled about the foundations of their new life in Christ. This will help them when others ridicule them that they are now serving the Lord or no longer doing things they used to do. They will know that those outside Christ need to know the Lord and that their lack of spiritual understanding makes them cooperative with the enemy.

THE IMPORTANCE OF SPIRITUAL UNDERSTANDING

If something goes wrong in their place of worship—which unfortunately does happen, such as wrong doctrine, betrayal from leadership, or hurt from brethren—they may leave the church and find somewhere else to fellowship. A believer with a good spiritual understanding of salvation will never be derailed by the enemy. They will stand their ground, knowing it is all about Jesus, not man. Man may fail and misrepresent the Lord, but the Lord remains faithful. Despite what man does, the truth remains that "God is light and in Him there is no darkness at all" (1 John 1:5). Everyone is an everlasting being and will one day spend eternity somewhere, depending on what they did with Jesus in this life. Heaven and Hell are real places, and the enemy is called "the wicked one" (1 John 5:18). God is always for us, and God is love (1 John 4:16). With this spiritual understanding, we know that the Lord is always the one to run to. The Lord is always an ever-present help (Psalm 46:1).

Yes, there are times that we will need encouragement and support, and this is where godly relationships come in. The Lord knows how to bring help our way.

Have you ever woken up in the morning and not felt like praying or reading the Bible? Spiritual understanding of why we need to pray, read, and meditate on God's Word will safeguard us from this trap. It's like you went to a doctor and were given medicine to use for a period. You know the side effects of not keeping up with your medicine. Whether you feel like it or not, you will take your medication. The world we live in is spiritual in nature. The Lord has given us tools to live in this life, one of which is prayer. The truth is, we cannot afford not to pray. We may need to ask for grace, but we cannot but pray, read, and meditate on the word of God daily.

If Hannah had not prayed, we might not have had Samuel. If David had not called on the Lord to help him fight Goliath, we may not have had the record in Scripture. If the saints had not prayed, Peter might have been killed. We have no idea how effective our prayers are.

We must choose our words carefully when we know that life and death are in the power of the tongue (Proverbs 18:21). Isn't it interesting that everyone is cautious with a knife because it can cause harm if not used correctly? Our words are equally important. We must watch what we say over our lives, cities, countries, other people, and loved ones.

How about eternal rewards? Did you know that the only thing that will follow us is our works (Revelation 14:13)? The scriptures tell us that we are labourers together with God (1 Corinthians 3:9). God equips, helps, empowers, and then rewards us. From Scripture, we can see one of the rewards for the twelve apostles of our Lord Jesus Christ. Did you know that the wall of the city has twelve foundations, and within them are the twelve apostles of the Lamb (Revelation 21:14)? This will remain there for eternity. They helped establish God's kingdom on earth and now see one of their eternal rewards. What is the Lord asking you to do? What do you have to give up to focus on what the Lord asks you to do? Is this temporary life worth giving up for eternal rewards? Yes, what you are led to do might not be popular, and you might even lose friends, but the cost is insignificant in comparison to the eternal rewards.

Paul put it this way:

"*For I consider that the sufferings of this present time are not worthy to be compared with the glory which shall be revealed in us*" (Romans 8:18).

Here is just a summary of the application of spiritual understanding.

Chapter 5
Conclusion

We live in a world with so many earthy demands. Social media has its advantages, but it also comes with a major problem: "distractions".

The most important thing every person needs to do is become "born again".

Jesus answered and said to him, "Most assuredly, I say to you, unless one is born [a]again, he cannot see the kingdom of God." ⁵ Jesus answered, "Most assuredly, I say to you, unless one is born of water and the Spirit, he cannot enter the kingdom of God. ⁶ That which is born of the flesh is flesh, and that which is born of the Spirit is spirit. ⁷ Do not marvel that I said to you, 'You must be born again (John 3:3, 5-7).

There is no other option. It is necessary to make Jesus Christ Lord and Saviour (Romans 10:9). It takes spiritual understanding to know the importance of this.

THE IMPORTANCE OF SPIRITUAL UNDERSTANDING

We have looked at a few areas of our Christian walk and now know the importance of spiritual understanding. God is a Spirit, and without spiritual understanding, we can easily procrastinate instead of dedicating the time required to more important spiritual values.

This is one reason wisdom and spiritual understanding are linked to walking worthy of the Lord unto all pleasing (Colossians 1:9-10).

We have looked at ways to acquire spiritual understanding, and one way is to study and meditate on the Word of God, allowing the Holy Spirit to open up the scriptures to us. The Book of Proverbs puts it this way: *"How much better is it to get wisdom than gold! And to get understanding is to be chosen rather than silver"* (Proverbs 16:16). This scripture tells us that "understanding" is to be chosen rather than silver, and in the content of what we are addressing here, "spiritual understanding" is of great value as it will help us live in this life from a heavenly perspective.

Now that we know the importance of spiritual understanding, we will pursue it and ask the Lord for help so we can indeed walk uprightly in this present world. We will also be able to encourage others, knowing that great rewards await them, if only they can see things from a heavenly perspective and pay the price necessary to apply what we have been given.

Although we have been given many spiritual tools to live in this life, effective application of these tools requires spiritual understanding.

Salvation Prayer

Father God, I come to you in Jesus' name. I admit that I am a sinner, and I now receive the sacrifice that Jesus Christ paid for me.

I confess with my mouth the Lord Jesus, and I believe in my heart that God raised Him from the dead.

I now declare that Jesus Christ is my Lord and Saviour.

Thank you, Father, for saving me in Jesus' name.

I am now your child. Amen.

If you've said this prayer for the first time, send an email to Bisiwriter@gmail.com . Start reading your Bible and ask the Lord to guide you to a good church.

About the author

Bisi Oladipupo has been a Christian for many years and lives in the United Kingdom with her family.

She has attended a few Bible colleges, and she has completed a diploma in Biblical Studies from a UK Bible college. She has also obtained an associate degree in Bible and Theology from a USA School of Ministry.

She is a teacher of God's Word, coordinates Bible studies, and a Christian fellowship.

Her author page is www.bisiwriter.com

She writes regularly, and her blog website is www.inspired-words.org

You can contact Bisi by email at bisiwriter@gmail.com

Also by Bisi

The Twelve Apostles of Jesus Christ: Lessons We Can Learn

The Lord's Cup in Communion: The Significance of taking the Lord's Supper

Different Ways to Receive Healing from Scripture and Walk in Health

Believing on The Name of Jesus Christ: What Every Believer Needs to Know

The Mind and Your Christian Walk: The Impact of the mind on our Christian walk

Relationship Skills in the Bible: Scriptural Principles of relating to others

The Nature of God's Kingdom: The Characteristics of the Kingdom of God

The Person of the Holy Spirit

BISI OLADIPUPO

41 Insights from the Book of Revelation

The Importance of Spiritual Discernment

God Speaks Through Nature

It's All About the Heart

A Better Covenant: A Look at the Covenants of God and Our Better Covenant

40 Day New Covenant Devotional

What Happens When We Pray?

Daily Bread for Healing: A 40-day Healing Devotional

40 Facts of Who Jesus Is: A Devotional

50 Prayers for Your Children and Generations to Come

The Grace of God: Why We Need It

THE IMPORTANCE OF SPIRITUAL UNDERSTANDING

www.ingramcontent.com/pod-product-compliance
Lightning Source LLC
Chambersburg PA
CBHW030046100526
44590CB00011B/341